W9-BUN-885

THE CHINESE HOROSCOPES LIBRARY

DOG

KWOK MAN-HO

DORLING KINDERSLEY
LONDON • NEW YORK • STUTTGART

A DORLING KINDERSLEY BOOK

Senior Editor — Sharon Lucas
Art Editor — Camilla Fox
Managing Editor — Krystyna Mayer
Managing Art Editor — Derek Coombes
DTP Designer — Doug Miller
Production Controller — Antony Heller
US Editor — Laaren Brown

Artworks: Danuta Mayer 4, 8, 11, 17, 27, 29, 31, 33, 35;
Giuliano Fornari 21; Studio Illibill 25; Jane Thomson; Sarah Ponder.

Special Photography by Steve Gorton. Thank you to The British Museum, Chinese Post
Office, Percival David Foundation of Chinese Art, and The Powell-Cotton Museum.

Additional Photography: Eric Crichton, Mike Dunning, Jo Foord, Steve Gorton, Stephen
Oliver, Tim Ridley, Clive Streeter.

Picture Credits: The British Museum 19tr; Courtesy of The Board of Trustees of the Victoria
& Albert Museum 15.

First American Edition, 1994
2 4 6 8 10 9 7 5 3 1

Published in the United States by Dorling Kindersley Publishing, Inc., 95 Madison Avenue,
New York, New York 10016

Copyright © 1994
Dorling Kindersley Limited, London
Text copyright © 1994 ICOREC

ISBN 1-56458-601-4
Library of Congress Catalog Number 93-48006

Reproduced by GRB Editrice, Verona, Italy
Printed and bound in Hong Kong by Imago

CONTENTS

INTRODUCING CHINESE HOROSCOPES

For thousands of years, the Chinese have used their astrology and religion to establish a harmony between people and the world around them.

The exact origins of the twelve animals of Chinese astrology – the Rat, Ox, Tiger, Rabbit, Dragon, Snake, Horse, Ram, Monkey, Rooster, Dog, and Pig – remain a mystery. Nevertheless, these animals are important in Chinese astrology. They are much more than general signposts to the year and to the possible good or bad times ahead for us all. The twelve animals of Chinese astrology are considered to be a reflection of the Universe itself.

YIN AND YANG

The many differences in our natures, moods, health, and fortunes reflect the wider changes within the Universe. The Chinese believe that every single thing in the Universe is held in balance by the dynamic, cosmic forces of yin and yang. Yin is feminine, watery, and cool; the force of the Moon and the rain. Yang is masculine, solid, and hot; the force of the Sun and the Earth. According to ancient Chinese belief, the concentrated essences of yin and yang became the four seasons, and the scattered essences of yin and yang became the myriad creatures that are found on Earth.

YIN AND YANG SYMBOL
White represents the female force of yin, and black represents the masculine force of yang.

The twelve animals of Chinese astrology are all associated with either yin or yang. The forces of yin rise as Winter approaches. These forces decline with the warmth of Spring, when yang begins to assert itself. Even in the course of a normal day, yin and yang are at work, constantly changing and balancing. These forces also naturally rise and fall within us all.

Everyone has their own internal balance of yin and yang. This affects our tempers, ambitions, and health. We also respond to the changes of weather, to the environment, and to the people who surround us.

THE FIVE ELEMENTS

All that we can touch, taste, or see is divided into five basic types or elements – wood, fire, earth, gold, and water. Everything in the Universe can be linked to one of these elements.

For example, the element earth is linked to four animals – the Ox, Dragon, Ram, and Dog. This element is also linked to the color yellow, sweet-tasting food, and the emotion of desire. The activity of these various elements indicates the fortune that may befall us.

AN INDIVIDUAL DISCOVERY

Chinese astrology can help you balance your yin and yang. It can also tell you which element you are, and the colors, tastes, parts of the body, or emotions that are linked to your particular sign. Your fortune can be prophesied according to the year, month, day, and hour in which you were born. You can identify the type of people to whom you are attracted, and the career that will suit your character. You can understand your changes of mood, your reactions to other places and to other people. In essence, you can start to discover what makes you an individual.

DIVINATION STICKS
Another ancient and popular method of Chinese fortune-telling is using special divination sticks to obtain a specific reading from prediction books.

CASTING YOUR HOROSCOPE

The Chinese calendar is based on the movement of the Moon, unlike the calendar used in the Western world, which is based on the movement of the Sun.

Before you begin to cast your Chinese horoscope, check your year of birth on the chart on pages 44 to 45. Check particularly carefully if you were born in the early months of the year. The Chinese year does not usually begin until January or February, and you might belong to the previous Chinese year. For example, if you were born in 1961 you might assume that you were born in the Year of the Ox. However, if your birthday falls before February 15 you belong to the previous Chinese year, which is the Year of the Rat.

THE SIXTY-YEAR CYCLE

The Chinese measure the passing of time by cycles of sixty years. The twelve astrological animals appear five times during the sixty-year cycle, and they appear in a slightly different form every time. For example, if you were born in 1934

you are a Dog on Guard, but if you were born in 1958, you are a Dog Going Onto the Mountain.

MONTHS, DAYS, AND HOURS

The twelve lunar months of the Chinese calendar do not correspond exactly with the twelve Western calendar months. This is because Chinese months are lunar, whereas Western months are solar. Chinese months are normally twenty-nine to thirty days long, and every three to four years an extra month is added to keep approximately in step with the Western year.

One Chinese hour is equal to two Western hours, and the twelve Chinese hours correspond to the twelve animal signs.

The year, month, day, and hour of birth are the keys to Chinese astrology. Once you know them, you can start to unlock your personal Chinese horoscope.

CHINESE ASTROLOGICAL WHEEL

In the center of the wheel is the yin and yang symbol. It is surrounded by the Chinese astrological character linked to each animal. The band of color indicates your element, and the outer ring reveals whether you are yin or yang.

Water

Earth

Wood

Fire

Gold

Yin

Yang

· DOG ·
MYTHS AND LEGENDS

*The Jade Emperor, heaven's ruler, asked to see the Earth's twelve
most interesting animals. When they arrived, he was impressed
by the Dog's intelligence, and awarded it eleventh place.*

There are many Chinese traditions and beliefs concerning the Dog. In the north, paper dogs were thrown into rivers on the fifth day of the fifth month in order to bite evil spirits and draw them away. Bodies of the dead were also given paper dogs for their protection. In the south and the west of China, it was believed that the Dog brought rice to humanity, and the Yao, a Chinese people, respected the Dog as their forefather. Elsewhere in China, suspected spirits were sprinkled with dog's blood in the belief that this would make them appear in their true form, and dreams of being bitten by a dog were interpreted as

SMILING TOMB DOG
*This earthenware dog was
discovered in a Chinese tomb
from the Six Dynasties.*

dead ancestors asking the living for some food. Dogs were very rarely given pet names, and even in present-day China, the names of pet dogs are usually foreign in origin rather than Chinese.

THE EMPEROR'S DOGS
The dog has always been considered humanity's best friend. However, the reverence and adoration bestowed upon the dogs of Emperor Ling Ti can have few parallels.

Ling Ti reigned in China from 168 to 189 AD. He loved dogs and considered them more intelligent and faithful than his own courtiers and officials. He made his most beloved dog an official of the Chin Hsien rank, the highest literary rank. This lucky dog was dressed in the full ceremonial robes and hat, which were specially altered to fit him. Like any faithful dog, he followed his master in the great processions and sat with him in Council. These remarkable privileges also extended to the dog's mate. She was given the status of a wife of a high-ranking official, which included her own human servants.

Finding that canine friends were much more enjoyable than human officials, Ling Ti appointed other dogs to various other official positions. As was by now the norm, these dogs were dressed in full ceremonial robes, and were also given servants.

The disbelief of Emperor Ling Ti's officials is unsurprising – barks from a dog invariably overruled their own carefully considered advice   but the dogs' opinions of the state of affairs are unfortunately unrecorded.

It would be unfair to suggest that Ling Ti was doggone crazy. He ruled successfully for over twenty years, so there was either method in his madness, or perhaps the dogs' advice was truly sound.

LION DOGS
These striking purple and turquoise figures are lion dogs. They were the trusted guardians of ancient Chinese temples.

· DOG ·
PERSONALITY

The Dog is completely trustworthy and faithful. It is always alert, not only to other people's needs and weaknesses, but also to its own.

You respond sympathetically when people are in need of your help, but are critical of those who are superficial, loud, or greedy. You do not suffer fools gladly, and if people step remotely out of line, your critical and witty tongue soon puts them firmly back in their place.

MOTIVATION

Regardless of the difficulties involved, you will always fight for the truth. You are adept at assessing information, which you use efficiently. At work, power games or aggressive behavior do not interest you in the slightest. Other people's well-being is what motivates you, and you are

sensitive to injustices. You are not driven by ambition or profit and are a steady worker for your own sense of satisfaction.

THE INNER DOG

Vulnerable and anxious by nature, you are always aware and critical of your own weaknesses. You are happiest when you are on familiar territory and tend to find most unknown situations rather daunting. Before starting any new ventures, you usually need someone to give you a helping hand and a boost to your self-confidence.

However, you are not timid in all areas of your life – you are never afraid to stand by the people who

DOG DETAIL
This vessel depicting a dog was discovered in a Chinese tomb from the Six Dynasties.

14

you care deeply for, and you have the ability to keep a cool head in times of trouble and distress.

There is a certain pessimistic streak within you, and you often suspect that catastrophes loom. However, all is not doom and gloom, and your pessimism tends to be fatalistic, rather than negative. If the worst happens, and your fears are realized, you are realistic, and accept this as the inevitable way of the world.

You have an alert and just nature and are a loyal companion. You are always true to your word and would never betray anyone who has put their trust in you.

Your sense of security is dependent on the atmosphere and the people around you. Consequently, you form deep and loyal attachments to your close friends.

You are an extremely conscientious and enthusiastic parent. Often you sacrifice your own needs in order to give yourself completely to the demands and well-being of your family.

THE DOG CHILD
The young Dog is very sensitive to its environment. It requires tender care and reassurance, and may need help to cope with its vulnerability.

EXPORTED DOG
Although the King Charles Spaniel is a British dog, this porcelain specimen with decoration in overglaze enamels is in fact late-18th-century Chinese exportware.

· DOG ·
LOVE

The Dog is a faithful, dependable creature. It seeks a secure relationship that is based on mutual respect and is not interested in romantic conquests or adventures.

Emotional matters can be troublesome for the Dog – you are sensitive and vulnerable, but sometimes have difficulty expressing the depth of your feelings. Consequently, you usually choose a relationship with someone you already know and trust.

Love can overwhelm your kind and gentle nature. However, if you discover glaring faults in your loved one, you have the good sense to end the relationship, despite the inevitable pain.

Your intuition is very strong, but you must beware of imagining feelings of indifference, or even infidelities, from your partner.

Ideally, you are suited to the Horse or the Tiger. If you allow the Horse sufficient freedom, it should make you happy. You are likely to have a mutual mental and physical attraction with the Tiger, and you could be highly supportive of each other.

The Ox, Rabbit, or another Dog will provide you with security and affection. You will want to devote yourself to the

GODDESS OF LOVE
Kuan Yin is a powerful figure in Chinese mythology. Once a male Buddhist deity, she is now known as the goddess of mercy, and as Sung-tzu, the giver of children.

CHINESE COMPATIBILITY WHEEL

Find your animal sign, then look for the animals that share its background color – the Dog has a blue background and is most compatible with the Tiger and the Horse. The symbol in the center of the wheel represents double happiness.

Ox, but may be disappointed by its lack of romanticism. The Rabbit will have to be treated gently – do not frighten it away with your idealistic schemes. You could settle down to enjoy a harmonious relationship with another Dog, but you will have to deal with your mutual suspicions first.

You may also find emotional happiness with the Snake or Pig. You will admire the Snake's wisdom, and it should make you feel secure. The Pig's optimistic nature could bring you immense happiness and serenity.

Relationships with the Dragon, Ram, Rooster, or Monkey are likely to be troubled. This is because the Dragon is too loud and superficial for your quiet and honest nature, while the Ram is a dreamer and worries almost as much as you. The Rooster is too harsh and critical, and the carefree Monkey may become bored by your idealism.

ORCHID

In China, the orchid, or Lan Hua, is an emblem of love and beauty. It is also a fertility symbol and represents many offspring.

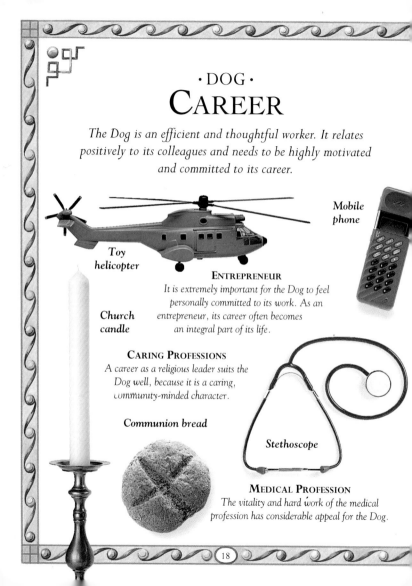

·DOG·
CAREER

The Dog is an efficient and thoughtful worker. It relates positively to its colleagues and needs to be highly motivated and committed to its career.

Mobile phone

Toy helicopter

Church candle

ENTREPRENEUR
It is extremely important for the Dog to feel personally committed to its work. As an entrepreneur, its career often becomes an integral part of its life.

CARING PROFESSIONS
A career as a religious leader suits the Dog well, because it is a caring, community-minded character.

Communion bread

Stethoscope

MEDICAL PROFESSION
The vitality and hard work of the medical profession has considerable appeal for the Dog.

Sheriff's badge

POLICE WORK

The Dog is interested in the law and ethics and is well suited to a policing career. It strives for peace and believes wholeheartedly in a job that makes the world a safer place.

Han dynasty tomb dog

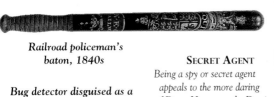

Railroad policeman's baton, 1840s

Bug detector disguised as a pen, and bugging device

SECRET AGENT

Being a spy or secret agent appeals to the more daring of Dogs. However, the Dog is only intent on seeking justice and is not attracted by the glamorous reputation of this career.

Magnifying glass

· DOG ·
HEALTH

Yin and yang are in a continual state of flux within the body. Good health is dependent upon the balance of yin and yang being constantly harmonious.

There is a natural minimum and maximum level of yin and yang in the human body. The body's energy is known as ch'i and is a yang force. The movement of ch'i in the human body is complemented by the movement of blood, which is a yin force. The very slightest displacement of the balance of yin or yang in the body can quickly lead to poor health and sickness. However, yang illness can be cured by yin treatment, and yin illness can be cured by yang treatment. Everybody has their own individual balance of yin and yang. It is likely that a hot-tempered person will have strong yang forces, and that a peaceful person will have strong yin forces. In Chinese medicine, your moods must be taken into account. A balance of joy, anger, sadness, happiness, worry, pensiveness, and fear must be maintained. This balance is known as the Harmony of the Seven Sentiments.

LINGCHIH FUNGUS
The fungus shown in this detail from a Ch'ing dynasty bowl is the "immortal" lingchih fungus, which symbolizes longevity.

SKULLCAP
This bitter-tasting herb can be used raw, sliced, or cooked in rice wine.

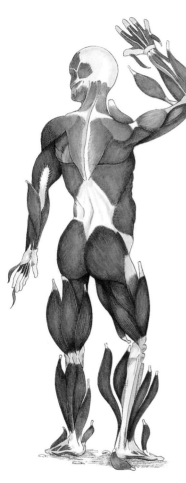

Born in the Year of the Dog, you are associated with the element earth. This element is linked with the spleen, pancreas, stomach, muscles, and mouth. These are the parts of the human body that are most relevant to the pattern of your health. You are also associated with the emotion of desire and with sweet-tasting food.

The herb skullcap (*Scutellaria*) is both yin and yang, and is associated with your Chinese astrological sign. Skullcap root can be used with honeysuckle and weeping forsythia to treat various forms of throat illness. When it is mixed with other ingredients, skullcap can be used to treat diverse ailments such as malaria, high blood pressure, painful abdomen, high temperature, headache, and delirium.

Chinese medicine is highly specific; therefore, never take skullcap or any other herb unless you are following professional advice from a fully qualified Chinese or Western doctor.

ASTROLOGY AND ANATOMY
Your element, earth, is associated with the digestive system. The stomach is a yang organ, and the pancreas, behind the stomach, is a yin organ.

· DOG ·
LEISURE

The Dog enjoys any wild landscapes and tranquil places that have an air of mystery. However, it is most content in peace and security, and is drawn to familiar environments.

Stopwatch

HORSEBACK RIDING
There is a reflective side to the Dog's nature, and it derives great pleasure from peace and quiet. Horseback riding is an excellent pastime for the Dog. On horseback, it is at one with both beast and nature. It can explore remote landscapes, and perhaps discover a derelict castle or ancient ruin.

RACING
The Dog dislikes being the center of attention, but enjoys the single-mindedness that racing demands. The glamour of the pursuit of speed does not interest the Dog in the slightest.

Riding gloves

Bridle

CAMPAIGNING

Although the Dog tries to avoid crowded places and unknown faces, it will happily attend parties if they are for a worthy cause. As long as the cause strikes a chord with the Dog's conscience, the Dog will be a tireless campaigner.

Party decorations

Rocking chair

Chinese scroll

RELAXING

The Dog has good taste and occasionally treats itself to luxury items, such as this Chinese scroll depicting Pekinese dogs. It enjoys relaxed evenings at home, where it can contemplate its latest tasteful acquisition in comfort.

· DOG ·
SYMBOLISM

In Chinese astrology, each of the twelve animals is linked with a certain food, direction, color, emotion, association, and symbol.

Ming dynasty bowl

COLOR

In China, fertile earth has a yellow hue. Yellow was the imperial color, worn by the emperor as the First Son of the Earth. Yellow is also linked with the Dog. This Chinese 16th-century bowl depicts a yellow lion dog.

FOOD

There are five tastes, according to Chinese astrology – salty, acrid, bitter, sweet, and sour. Sweet foods, such as cashews, are associated with the Dog.

Cashews

Antique
Chinese
compass

**Section of a
map of Rome**

DIRECTION
*The Chinese compass points south, whereas
the Western compass points north. The
Chinese compass has an extra direction,
the center, which is the Dog's direction.*

ASSOCIATION
*The capital city and its life are
linked with the Dog.*

SYMBOL
*The Dog's symbol is the plumb line, which is
used to measure the depth of water.*

Plumb line

*Baby
expressing
desire*

EMOTION
*Desire is the emotion that is
connected with the Dog.*

DOG ON GUARD

~ 1934 1994 ~

The Dog personality combines "dogged" determination with considerable personal insecurity. Luckily, the Dog on Guard has much of this tension under control.

Even though you invariably know your own potential, your sense of insecurity may often hold you back. Because you are associated with a bud breaking forth, however, you have the possibility of breaking out of this insecurity.

This means that you always have the potential to make a good life for yourself, although this relies upon your being able to learn to control the difficult aspects of being a Dog on Guard.

PERSONALITY

All Dogs believe strongly in what they consider to be right, and you are particularly tenacious in an argument. You cannot endure injustice or deception.

You are a fierce debater and upholder of everything that is right and proper. This can lead you to being swift to accuse others and slow to hear the other side of an argument. This tendency could upset many people who might otherwise agree with you.

Learn to balance your sense of conviction with a willingness to listen to other people, rather than just hearing them. This should make you a more attractive personality. Do not be too hard on yourself, for a sense of balance does not necessarily mean that you have abandoned your side of the argument.

Throughout your life you are likely to express two strong aspects of your personality, consisting of the public and the private sides.

In public you are gregarious, lively, and intensely involved with others. In private, however, you are much quieter and considerably less confident. You have a tendency to brood when you are inactive. You may try to lose yourself in action,

Dog on Guard

when it might be best to allow
yourself time to sit and think. Try to
learn to make the most of these
different, but complementary,
aspects of your personality.

PROSPECTS

Because of your skills and sense of
determination, you should achieve
considerable success both at work
and in your social life.

You could sometimes find that your
reflective personality makes you
loathe the external world of success.
Try not to despise success, and make
every effort to keep these feelings in
a sensible perspective.

Once you have decided upon
what is important and have put your
wealth within a wider framework of
reference, you should find it easier
to enjoy your comforts.

SLEEPY DOG

~ 1946 2006 ~

*This Dog's relaxed image is emphasized by its association
with a domestic fire, glowing on the hearth. Consequently,
it is likely to have a comfortable life.*

You are a very secure Dog – you have made a role for yourself in society and can happily rest in your dwelling place. However, most Dogs experience some difficulties in expressing emotion, and if this trait becomes fused with your relaxed personality, it could cause significant problems for you and for others.

You could become thoughtless and could cause considerable emotional distress to yourself, your partner, and your family.

FEMALE CHARACTERISTICS

Because of the calming effects of the yin influence, the female Sleepy Dog is a particularly fortunate creature. Invariably, she should enjoy success in her professional and personal life, and she is also likely to be highly respected. She should be able to enjoy a high income and sustain a good lifestyle.

YOUTH

All Sleepy Dogs are likely to enjoy a relatively easy life from their earliest days. Your youth will probably be a period of calm. School is not likely to cause problems for you, even though you are rarely willing to make a tremendous effort.

CAREER

Initially, your working life should progress smoothly, but there is likely to come a time when it will be necessary to take a significant leap in your career.

Do not be satisfied with lying back and waiting for things to happen, for your opportunity might easily pass you by. It is up to you to always look for people who might be in positions to help your endeavors. If you work thoughtfully and cleverly, you should find that these people can help you considerably.

Sleepy Dog

FRIENDSHIPS

You are always likely to be popular, but in times of trouble, you may discover that some of your friends may suddenly become hard to find. Take the time to observe who your true friends are, and once you have identified them, be sure always to stay loyal.

FAMILY

Parenthood suits your personality, but beware of your characteristic "dogged" loyalty. Your natural instinct is to spring to the defense of your family, but sometimes you may need to remain more objective. Even if other people are saying painful things about your family, try to allow them to express their opinions.

Others do not necessarily share your blinding sense of loyalty and may be able to see things within your family that you cannot.

RELATIONSHIPS

In your committed relationship, you are likely to be very content. However, always try to work on your problem with expressing emotions. As long as you manage to balance your personality, you should find that you have a very good committed relationship.

DOG GOING ONTO THE MOUNTAIN

~ 1958 2018 ~

This is the typical Dog — trusting and extremely loyal. It is associated with reaping what is sown, which highlights the fullest expression of the Dog personality.

You often appear to be vigorous and confident when you actually feel insecure and hesitant. You may consider this to be a weakness, but you will only be weakened if you give in to your fear.

PERSONALITY

You defend anything that you consider to be true and right. You tend to loathe injustice and are not afraid to fight any wrongs.

Your kind nature is extremely attractive, and you will gladly give yourself to your friends and to those you love. However, sometimes you may feel overwhelmed, even though others are likely to perceive you as a pillar of strength.

Because you are so independent, your life is bound to be difficult at times. Even though you have the friendship and admiration of many

people, you are also likely to make some powerful enemies. Since you are unlikely to be afraid of standing up to people in authority, they might become suspicious of you.

YOUTH

During school and your early years at work, your independence is unlikely to bring you conventional success. However, you are invariably sowing precious seeds of trust and friendship that should bring you plenty of rewards later in life.

CAREER

As you grow older, you should find that the people who have been helped by you will want to reciprocate, for they will often have achieved their success as a direct consequence of your support. You should reach a prosperous position.

Dog Going Onto the Mountain

RELATIONSHIPS

Unfortunately, your innate lack of confidence could cause problems in your emotional life. At some point, you will probably have to take the significant risk of asking someone to share their life with you. Even though you may feel personally inadequate, always try to summon up your courage, and be prepared to feel surprised by the results.

PROSPECTS

People who frequently fight injustice sometimes develop an overriding sense of self-importance and arrogance. You, however, can easily use your lack of confidence to your best advantage.

If you learn to combine your natural fervor with your quiet inner voice, you have the potential to become a truly strong person.

TEMPLE DOG

~ 1910 1970 ~

This Dog lives in a place of worship. Unfortunately, there are those who would violate this holy place, and it is the Temple Dog's task to defend it at all costs.

You are associated with holding two things at once, symbolizing balancing two conflicting dimensions in tension. This means that essentially, your life is likely to be happy, but you should always be prepared to overcome some disasters.

PERSONALITY
These disasters are likely to arise from your personality and will probably occur fairly early in your life. You tend to be outspoken and fearless, especially in defense of anything that you value and respect. Unfortunately, this means that you are likely to put yourself into situations from which it is difficult to extract yourself.

Sometimes it may feel as if these situations are about to overwhelm you. However, as long as you stay true to yourself, you should find the strength to work through them and survive. Invariably, these troubles will leave you wiser and more mature. Perhaps they should be perceived as a blessing, for they will eventually help you develop into a better person.

Do not allow the typical Dog trait of moodiness to worry you unduly. It is probably best to look on it as a characteristic that you simply have to live with. Remember that your moods are only likely to be a weakness if you allow them to make you feel unnecessarily insecure.

FEMALE CHARACTERISTICS
Because of the calming and soothing effects of the yin influence, the female Temple Dog should be able to enjoy a much easier life than the male. Although the female will undoubtedly have to face problems and difficulties, her life should eventually prove to be prosperous.

Temple Dog

PROSPECTS

All Temple Dogs are likely to need considerable maturity and wisdom, for at some point in your life an important challenge will have to be faced. There is no avoiding this challenge, but you can prepare yourself for it.

It may be hard at first, but try to beware of someone you trust, someone who seems quiet and unthreatening. This person could suddenly cause you immense problems. If you manage to handle this situation with understanding and firmness, you should not suffer too great a loss or difficulty, but it will nevertheless be a significant test of your maturity.

You will probably always perceive convention to be an empty form and may consequently find social occasions a source of stress. Try to retain your critical edge, but also learn to relax whenever possible. Do not be too hard on yourself – remember that you do not have to fight against everything in life that is not as honest or as meaningful as you would prefer.

FAMILY DOG

~ 1922 1982 ~

*You are the typical kind and generous Dog. You are
associated with making offerings to the gods or ancestors,
and enjoying the subsequent rewards.*

You possess an innate kindness, which arises spontaneously from your generous nature. Although your early life is likely to be fairly impoverished, you should be well rewarded in your later years.

PERSONALITY
Your greatest skill is the ability to keep a cool head. You do not allow anything to get out of proportion. Even though you are far from cynical about life, you also accept that it consists of ups and downs. This realistic attitude allows you to keep yourself on a fairly even keel.

You will gladly help anyone in trouble and will use your own scarce financial resources to help others. However, you are never likely to be in need yourself. It may seem strange, but your money supply is far more likely to dry up if you stifle your generosity.

However, because of your great generosity and willingness to help others, you will probably not be financially comfortable. You will have to work very hard to support yourself and your family. Although money is unlikely to be absent entirely, it may always be slightly too scarce for comfort.

Luckily, this situation is increasingly likely to change as you grow older. You should find that the people you have helped in the past will repay you, perhaps in ways that you could never have thought possible. After your middle age, you are never likely to be in need and should at last be able to take a break from your hard work.

CAREER
In your professional life, it is likely that people in authority have been watching you steadily grow in

Family Dog

maturity and ability. Their observations should lead to a full appreciation of your kind nature and essential worth.

As a result, you should be considered as someone to be relied upon, and worthy of promotion. You will certainly have worked very hard over the years for this success, so do your best to enjoy your rewards when they come.

PROSPECTS

Even though you are likely to be engaged in many people's sorrows and difficulties during your youth, you should still have an optimistic outlook on life. During your middle years, this outlook could tarnish at the edges, because your life might seem to be an unceasing struggle. However, you should find that life is eventually good to you.

YOUR CHINESE
MONTH OF BIRTH

*Find the table with your year of birth, and see where your
birthday falls. For example, if you were born on
August 30, 1958, you were born in Chinese month 7.*

1 You are a solid and fastidious worker. You are intellectually bright, but beware of obstinacy.

2 You invariably succeed in life. You are not frightened to fight for what you believe is right.

3 Your actions are sometimes misunderstood by others. You are sensitive and suffer mood swings.

4 You are hardworking, but your occasional underhanded methods could destroy your good fortune.

5 You care too much for people, and their sufferings become your own. Try to be more objective.

6 You are fit, vigorous, and lucky. You will be most successful working as your own boss.

7 You have great drive, but can be deceitful. Try to develop your honesty and determination instead.

8 You are clever and learn from other people. However, try to control your pride and your greed.

9 You are full of bright ideas, but nothing seems to come to fruition. Learn to be more methodical.

10 You could enjoy a life of fame, but you need to stop daydreaming and concentrate on the present.

11 Sometimes you may seem to be surrounded by opponents. Try to find some trustworthy friends.

12 You work hard, but tend to be inconsiderate. Beware, for success without friendship can be lonely.

* Some Chinese years contain double months:	
1922: Month 5	1982: Month 4
May 27 – June 24	April 24 – May 22
June 25 – July 23	May 23 – June 20
2006: Month 7	
July 25 – Aug 23	
Aug 24 – Sept 21	

1910	
Feb 10 – March 10	1
March 11 – April 9	2
April 10 – May 8	3
May 9 – June 6	4
June 7 – July 6	5
July 7 – Aug 4	6
Aug 5 – Sept 3	7
Sept 4 – Oct 2	8
Oct 3 – Nov 1	9
Nov 2 – Dec 1	10
Dec 2 – Dec 31	11
Jan 1 1911 – Jan 29	12

1922	
Jan 28 – Feb 26	1
Feb 27 – March 27	2
March 28 – April 26	3
April 27 – May 26	4
See double months box	5
July 24 – Aug 22	6
Aug 23 – Sept 20	7
Sept 21 – Oct 19	8
Oct 20 – Nov 18	9
Nov 19 – Dec 17	10
Dec 18 – Jan 16 1923	11
Jan 17 – Feb 15	12

1934	
Feb 14 – March 14	1
March 15 – April 13	2
April 14 – May 12	3
May 13 – June 11	4
June 12 – July 11	5
July 12 – Aug 9	6
Aug 10 – Sept 8	7
Sept 9 – Oct 7	8
Oct 8 – Nov 6	9
Nov 7 – Dec 6	10
Dec 7 – Jan 4 1935	11
Jan 5 – Feb 3	12

1946	
Feb 2 – March 3	1
March 4 – April 1	2
April 2 – April 30	3
May 1 – May 30	4
May 31 – June 28	5
June 29 – July 27	6
July 28 – Aug 26	7
Aug 27 – Sept 24	8
Sept 25 – Oct 24	9
Oct 25 – Nov 23	10
Nov 24 – Dec 22	11
Dec 23 – Jan 21 1947	12

1958	
Feb 18 – March 19	1
March 20 – April 18	2
April 19 – May 18	3
May 19 – June 16	4
June 17 – July 16	5
July 17 – Aug 14	6
Aug 15 – Sept 12	7
Sept 13 – Oct 12 ————	8
Oct 13 – Nov 10	9
Nov 11 – Dec 10	10
Dec 11 – Jan 8 1959	11
Jan 9 – Feb 7	12

1970	
Feb 6 – March 7	1
March 8 – April 5	2
April 6 – May 4	3
May 5 – June 3	4
June 4 – July 2	5
July 3 – Aug 1	6
Aug 2 – Aug 31	7
Sept 1 – Sept 29	8
Sept 30 – Oct 29	9
Oct 30 – Nov 28	10
Nov 29 – Dec 27	11
Dec 28 – Jan 26 1971	12

1982	
Jan 25 – Feb 23	1
Feb 24 – March 24	2
March 25 – April 23	3
See double months box	4
June 21 – July 20	5
July 21 – Aug 18	6
Aug 19 – Sept 16	7
Sept 17 – Oct 16	8
Oct 17 – Nov 14	9
Nov 15 – Dec 14	10
Dec 15 – Jan 13 1983	11
Jan 14 – Feb 12	12

1994	
Feb 10 – March 11	1
March 12 – April 10	2
April 11 – May 10	3
May 11 – June 8	4
June 9 – July 8	5
July 9 – Aug 7	6
Aug 8 – Sept 5	7
Sept 6 – Oct 4	8
Oct 5 – Nov 2	9
Nov 3 – Dec 1	10
Dec 2 – Dec 31	11
Jan 1 – Jan 30 1995	12

2006	
Jan 29 – Feb 27	1
Feb 28 – March 28	2
March 29 – April 27	3
April 28 – May 26	4
May 27 – June 25	5
June 26 – July 24	6
See double months box	7
Sept 22 – Oct 21	8
Oct 22 – Nov 20	9
Nov 21 – Dec 19	10
Dec 20 – Jan 18 2007	11
Jan 19 – Feb 17	12

YOUR CHINESE
DAY OF BIRTH

Refer to the previous page to discover the beginning of your Chinese month of birth, then use the chart below to calculate your Chinese day of birth.

If you were born on May 5, 1910, your birthday is in the month starting on April 10. Find 10 on the chart below. Using 10 as the first day, count the days until you reach the date of your birthday. (Remember that not all months contain 31 days.) You were born on day 26 of the Chinese month.

If you were born in a Chinese double month, simply count the days from the first date of the month that contains your birthday.

1	2	3	4	5	6	7
8	9	10	11	12	13	14
15	16	17	18	19	20	21
22	23	24	25	26	27	28
29	30	31				

DAY 1, 10, 19, OR 28
You are trustworthy and set high standards, but tend to rush your

projects. Try to be cautious, and do not be too self-obsessed. You may receive unexpected money but must control your spending. You are suited to a career in the public sector or the arts.

DAY 2, 11, 20, OR 29
You are honest and popular. You need peace, but also require lively company. You are prone to outbursts of temper. You tend to enjoy life and make the most of your opportunities. You are suited to a literary or artistic career.

DAY 3, 12, 21, OR 30
You are quick-witted, but may appear to be difficult. As a result, people may be wary of being your friend. You have a disciplined character and fight for the truth. You are suited to careers that have a competitive element.

DAY 4, 13, 22, OR 31

You are very warmhearted, but also have a reserved attitude, which can sometimes make you appear unapproachable. If you try to be more outgoing and sociable, you should become more popular. You have a calm and patient manner, and are suited to a career as an academic or researcher.

DAY 5, 14, OR 23

Your fiery, obstinate nature can sometimes make it difficult for you to accept suggestions or opinions from others, and your stubbornness may lead to quarrels or problems. You should be lucky with money and may often use your profits to set up new projects. Your innate intelligence will enable you to cope with a demanding career.

DAY 6, 15, OR 24

You have an open, stable, and cheerful character, and enjoy an active social life. You are affectionate and emotional, and have a tendency to daydream. This can lead to confusion, and your eagerness to help others may be stifled by your indecision. Although you will never be wealthy, you should always have enough money.

DAY 7, 16, OR 25

You enjoy a certain amount of excitement in your life, but must learn to become more realistic and disciplined. Although you are a natural performer, you should beware of alienating your friends or colleagues. In your career, the opportunity to travel is more important to you than a good salary or a high standard of living.

DAY 8, 17, OR 26

You have very good judgment, but should not act too quickly. Your social skills may sometimes be lacking, and you may alienate other people, so try to be more tactful. You will experience poverty, but also wealth. Your calm and determined nature is combined with a free spirit, making you best suited to self-employment.

DAY 9, 18, OR 27

You are happy, optimistic, and warmhearted. You keep yourself busy and are rarely troubled by trivialities. Occasionally you quarrel unnecessarily with your friends, and it is important for you to learn to control your moods. You are particularly suited to a career as a sole owner or proprietor.

YOUR CHINESE
HOUR OF BIRTH

In Chinese time, one hour is equal to two Western hours.
Each Chinese double hour is associated with one of the
twelve astrological animals.

11 P.M. – 1 A.M. RAT HOUR
You are independent and have a hot temper. Try to think before you speak. Your thrifty nature will be useful in business and at home. You are willing to help those who are close to you, and they will return your support.

1 – 3 A.M. OX HOUR
Up to the age of twenty, your life could be difficult, but your fortunes are likely to improve after these troublesome years. In your career, be prepared to take a risk or to leave home during your youth to achieve your goals. You should enjoy a prosperous old age.

3 – 5 A.M. TIGER HOUR
You have a lively and creative nature, which may cause family arguments in your youth. Between the ages of twenty and forty you may have many problems. Luckily, your fortunes are likely to improve dramatically in your forties.

5 – 7 A.M. RABBIT HOUR
Your parents should be helpful, but your siblings may be your rivals. You may have to move away from home to achieve your full potential at work. Your committed relationship may take time to become settled, but you should get along much better with everyone after middle age.

7 – 9 A.M. DRAGON HOUR
You have a quick-witted, determined, and attractive nature. Your life will be busy, but you could sometimes be lonely. You should achieve a good standard of living. Try to curb your excessive self-confidence, for it could make working relationships difficult.

9 – 11 A.M. SNAKE HOUR

You have a talent for business and should find it easy to build your career and provide for your family. You have a very generous spirit and will gladly help your friends when they are in trouble. Unfortunately, family relationships are unlikely to run smoothly.

11 A.M. – 1 P.M. HORSE HOUR

You are active, clever, and obstinate. Try to listen to advice. You are fascinated with travel and with changing your life. Learn to control your extravagance, for it could lead to financial suffering.

1 – 3 P.M. RAM HOUR

Steady relationships with your family, friends, or partners are difficult, because you have an active nature. You are clever, but must not force your views on others. Your fortunes will be at their lowest in your middle age.

3 – 5 P.M. MONKEY HOUR

You earn and spend money easily. Your character is attractive, but frustrating, too. Sometimes your parents are not able to give you adequate moral support. Your committed relationship should be good, but do not brood over emotional problems for too long – if you do your career could suffer.

5 – 7 P.M. ROOSTER HOUR

In your teenage years you may have many arguments with your family. There could even be a family division, which should eventually be resolved. You are trustworthy, kind, and warmhearted, and never intend to hurt other people.

7 – 9 P.M. DOG HOUR

Your brave, capable, hard-working nature is ideally suited to self-employment, and the forecast for your career is excellent. Try to control your impatience and vanity. The quality of your life is far more important to you than the amount of money you have saved.

9 – 11 P.M. PIG HOUR

You are particularly skilled at manual work and always set yourself high standards. Although you are warmhearted, you do not like to surround yourself with too many friends. However, the people who are close to you have your complete trust. You can be easily upset by others, but are able to forgive and forget quickly.

YOUR FORTUNE IN OTHER ANIMAL YEARS

The Dog's fortunes fluctuate during the twelve animal years. It is best to concentrate on a year's positive aspects, and to take care when faced with the seemingly negative.

YEAR OF THE RAT
Although the Year of the Rat is generally a good year for the Dog, you should make an effort to be calm and sensible. It would be unwise to tempt fate too much this year; therefore, try to keep any sense of overconfidence under control.

YEAR OF THE OX
Indecision and a sense of uncertainty will dominate your response to other people and events in the Year of the Ox. The best way to survive this constant state of quandary is to relax and to try to conduct yourself at a reasonably steady pace.

YEAR OF THE TIGER
Unfortunately, a friend is likely to turn against you this year. As a result, you may have troubles in various areas of your life. Luckily, your more trustworthy friends should offer you love and support.

YEAR OF THE RABBIT
This is a very good time for the Dog, because various areas of your life are highly auspicious in the Year of the Rabbit. You are likely to be successful in anything that you decide to try your hand at, and you may even become famous.

YEAR OF THE DRAGON
After last year's excess of success, it was perhaps inevitable that the Year of the Dragon would be a year of negativity. There is little you can do to improve your fortune, and it will probably be best if you lie low and wait for better times.

YEAR OF THE SNAKE

Your potential for success is considerable during the Year of the Snake. There could be a high price to pay, however, in the form of personal compromise. Be on guard against this, and do not allow yourself to be overwhelmed by your greed.

YEAR OF THE HORSE

Various difficulties could be experienced in your family life in the Year of the Horse. Luckily, you can escape these problems by concentrating on your professional life. This should be much easier, and you could enjoy a certain amount of success.

YEAR OF THE RAM.

You are likely to be confronted with many problems during the Year of the Ram, particularly at its start. However, you are a creature of "dogged" resolve and determination, and these useful traits should invariably ensure your survival.

YEAR OF THE MONKEY

This is an intensely sociable year. Your life should be a hub of activity, and there will be many opportunities to socialize at parties. This is all very enjoyable, but you will have to look after your health in order to sustain your energy.

YEAR OF THE ROOSTER

Although you may be bombarded with troubles in all areas of your life during this year, you must not allow this to depress you. Instead, try to retain a sense of positivity, keep a low profile, and stay calm.

YEAR OF THE DOG

This is a time of mixed fortunes. You are likely to experience a nagging sense of frustration throughout the Year of the Dog, but luckily, your social life is varied and excellent and should more than compensate for any irritating difficulties.

YEAR OF THE PIG

A surprising gift of money should make you very happy in the Year of the Pig. It is a year of desperate trouble for many people, but your good fortune should ensure that you invariably succeed in areas where others fail.

YOUR CHINESE
YEAR OF BIRTH

*Your astrological animal corresponds to the Chinese year of
your birth. It is the single most important key in the quest
to unlock your Chinese horoscope.*

Find your Western year of birth in
the left-hand column of the chart.
Your Chinese astrological animal is
on the same line as your year of birth
in the right-hand column of the
chart. If you were born in the
beginning of the year, check the

middle column of the chart carefully.
For example, if you were born in
1971, you might assume that you
belong to the Year of the Pig.
However, if your birthday falls
before January 27, you actually
belong to the Year of the Dog.

1900	Jan 31 – Feb 18, 1901	Rat	1917	Jan 23 – Feb 10, 1918	Snake
1901	Feb 19 – Feb 7, 1902	Ox	1918	Feb 11 – Jan 31, 1919	Horse
1902	Feb 8 – Jan 28, 1903	Tiger	1919	Feb 1 – Feb 19, 1920	Ram
1903	Jan 29 – Feb 15, 1904	Rabbit	1920	Feb 20 – Feb 7, 1921	Monkey
1904	Feb 16 – Feb 3, 1905	Dragon	1921	Feb 8 – Jan 27, 1922	Rooster
1905	Feb 4 – Jan 24, 1906	Snake	1922	Jan 28 – Feb 15, 1923	Dog
1906	Jan 25 – Feb 12, 1907	Horse	1923	Feb 16 – Feb 4, 1924	Pig
1907	Feb 13 – Feb 1, 1908	Ram	1924	Feb 5 – Jan 23, 1925	Rat
1908	Feb 2 – Jan 21, 1909	Monkey	1925	Jan 24 – Feb 12, 1926	Ox
1909	Jan 22 – Feb 9, 1910	Rooster	1926	Feb 13 – Feb 1, 1927	Tiger
1910	Feb 10 – Jan 29, 1911	Dog	1927	Feb 2 – Jan 22, 1928	Rabbit
1911	Jan 30 – Feb 17, 1912	Pig	1928	Jan 23 – Feb 9, 1929	Dragon
1912	Feb 18 – Feb 5, 1913	Rat	1929	Feb 10 – Jan 29, 1930	Snake
1913	Feb 6 – Jan 25, 1914	Ox	1930	Jan 30 – Feb 16, 1931	Horse
1914	Jan 26 – Feb 13, 1915	Tiger	1931	Feb 17 – Feb 5, 1932	Ram
1915	Feb 14 – Feb 2, 1916	Rabbit	1932	Feb 6 – Jan 25, 1933	Monkey
1916	Feb 3 – Jan 22, 1917	Dragon	1933	Jan 26 – Feb 13, 1934	Rooster

1934	Feb 14 – Feb 3, 1935	Dog	1971	Jan 27 – Feb 14, 1972	Pig
1935	Feb 4 – Jan 23, 1936	Pig	1972	Feb 15 – Feb 2, 1973	Rat
1936	Jan 24 – Feb 10, 1937	Rat	1973	Feb 3 – Jan 22, 1974	Ox
1937	Feb 11 – Jan 30, 1938	Ox	1974	Jan 23 – Feb 10, 1975	Tiger
1938	Jan 31 – Feb 18, 1939	Tiger	1975	Feb 11 – Jan 30, 1976	Rabbit
1939	Feb 19 – Feb 7, 1940	Rabbit	1976	Jan 31 – Feb 17, 1977	Dragon
1940	Feb 8 – Jan 26, 1941	Dragon	1977	Feb 18 – Feb 6, 1978	Snake
1941	Jan 27 – Feb 14, 1942	Snake	1978	Feb 7 – Jan 27, 1979	Horse
1942	Feb 15 – Feb 4, 1943	Horse	1979	Jan 28 – Feb 15, 1980	Ram
1943	Feb 5 – Jan 24, 1944	Ram	1980	Feb 16 – Feb 4, 1981	Monkey
1944	Jan 25 – Feb 12, 1945	Monkey	1981	Feb 5 – Jan 24, 1982	Rooster
1945	Feb 13 – Feb 1, 1946	Rooster	1982	Jan 25 – Feb 12, 1983	Dog
1946	Feb 2 – Jan 21, 1947	Dog	1983	Feb 13 – Feb 1, 1984	Pig
1947	Jan 22 – Feb 9, 1948	Pig	1984	Feb 2 – Feb 19, 1985	Rat
1948	Feb 10 – Jan 28, 1949	Rat	1985	Feb 20 – Feb 8, 1986	Ox
1949	Jan 29 – Feb 16, 1950	Ox	1986	Feb 9 – Jan 28, 1987	Tiger
1950	Feb 17 – Feb 5, 1951	Tiger	1987	Jan 29 – Feb 16, 1988	Rabbit
1951	Feb 6 – Jan 26, 1952	Rabbit	1988	Feb 17 – Feb 5, 1989	Dragon
1952	Jan 27 – Feb 13, 1953	Dragon	1989	Feb 6 – Jan 26, 1990	Snake
1953	Feb 14 – Feb 2, 1954	Snake	1990	Jan 27 – Feb 14, 1991	Horse
1954	Feb 3 – Jan 23, 1955	Horse	1991	Feb 15 – Feb 3, 1992	Ram
1955	Jan 24 – Feb 11, 1956	Ram	1992	Feb 4 – Jan 22, 1993	Monkey
1956	Feb 12 – Jan 30, 1957	Monkey	1993	Jan 23 – Feb 9, 1994	Rooster
1957	Jan 31 – Feb 17, 1958	Rooster	1994	Feb 10 – Jan 30, 1995	Dog
1958	Feb 18 – Feb 7, 1959	Dog	1995	Jan 31 – Feb 18, 1996	Pig
1959	Feb 8 – Jan 27, 1960	Pig	1996	Feb 19 – Feb 6, 1997	Rat
1960	Jan 28 – Feb 14, 1961	Rat	1997	Feb 7 – Feb 27, 1998	Ox
1961	Feb 15 – Feb 4, 1962	Ox	1998	Jan 28 – Feb 15, 1999	Tiger
1962	Feb 5 – Jan 24, 1963	Tiger	1999	Feb 16 – Feb 4, 2000	Rabbit
1963	Jan 25 – Feb 12, 1964	Rabbit	2000	Feb 5 – Jan 23, 2001	Dragon
1964	Feb 13 – Feb 1, 1965	Dragon	2001	Jan 24 – Feb 11, 2002	Snake
1965	Feb 2 – Jan 20, 1966	Snake	2002	Feb 12 – Jan 31, 2003	Horse
1966	Jan 21 – Feb 8, 1967	Horse	2003	Feb 1 – Jan 21, 2004	Ram
1967	Feb 9 – Jan 29, 1968	Ram	2004	Jan 22 – Feb 8, 2005	Monkey
1968	Jan 30 – Feb 16, 1969	Monkey	2005	Feb 9 – Jan 28, 2006	Rooster
1969	Feb 17 – Feb 5, 1970	Rooster	2006	Jan 29 – Feb 17, 2007	Dog
1970	Feb 6 – Jan 26, 1971	Dog	2007	Feb 18 – Feb 6, 2008	Pig